Real Life: Artists

Written by Michael Cox

Contents

T0345639

Painters express themselves and the way they see the world in many different ways.

Artists are people who create works of art. Art can be anything that makes us look at the world more closely, or in different ways. Some artists make music or films, some dance or perform on stage, and others write books.

Painters create art that can be looked at rather than listened to or read. They may paint or draw pictures of what they see in the world around them, or use their imagination to dream up something new. Sculptors make three-dimensional (3D) art using clay, stone and other materials.

The four artists in this book lived in very different parts of the world at very different times, but they've got lots in common. They were all **creative** people, who were interested in everything they saw and experienced. They expressed how they felt about the world through their art.

The artists in this book created an amazing amount of art that has been seen by millions of people, helping them to see things in new ways. But don't take our word for it. Read about the artists, enjoy their creations ... then make up your own mind.

Leonardo da Vinci

FACT FILE

- **Name:** Leonardo da Vinci
- **Date of birth:** 15th April 1452
- **Nationality:** Italian
- **Died:** 2nd May 1519
- **Famous for:** painting, **sculpture**, **architecture**, inventing and science
- **Most famous works of art:** *Mona Lisa*, *The Last Supper*, and *Vitruvian Man*
- **Strange but true:** Leonardo was a practical joker who made stink bombs out of rotten fish!

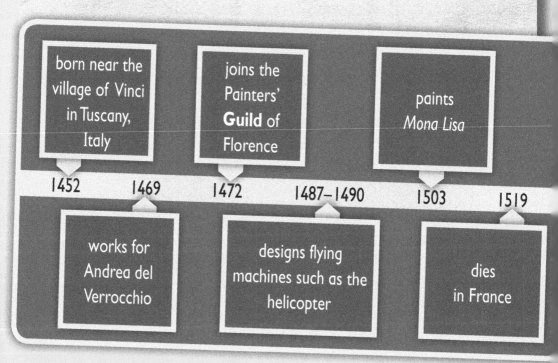

born near the village of Vinci in Tuscany, Italy — 1452

joins the Painters' **Guild** of Florence — 1472

paints *Mona Lisa* — 1503

works for Andrea del Verrocchio — 1469

designs flying machines such as the helicopter — 1487–1490

dies in France — 1519

A Keen Scribbler

Leonardo da Vinci was born near the Tuscan village of Vinci in Italy. His father was a lawyer and his mother was a 16-year-old country girl. Growing up, Leonardo sketched the local countryside, carrying a pencil and drawing pad wherever he went. He thought that drawing helped him to see and understand the world in more detail.

The countryside of Vinci has changed very little since Leonardo was a boy.

During his life, Leonardo produced an amazing 13,000 pages of notes and sketches. He wrote down almost all of his thoughts in mirror writing!

5

The Young Artist

When Leonardo was 15 years old, he and his family moved to Florence. He began working as an **apprentice** to the famous artist, Andrea del Verrocchio, in 1469. Leonardo learned how to mix colours, prepare canvases and make paintbrushes. He also practised his own painting and drawing. After two years, Andrea made Leonardo his assistant.

One day, Andrea asked Leonardo to paint one of the angels in a picture he was working on. He was so impressed by Leonardo's work that he was tempted to "give up painting forever!"

Florence was a brilliant place for a young artist to be. It was a city full of new art, poetry, architecture and science.

The city of Florence.

The Enormous Clay Horse

By 1482, Leonardo's fame was growing, and he left Florence for Milan. He was employed by the Duke of Milan to build a seven-metre high **bronze** statue of a horse. It took him ten years just to finish the clay model from which the bronze statue would be **cast**. Then, in 1494, France invaded Italy, and the Duke used all the bronze to make cannons!

The horse was finally cast in 1998 based on Leonardo's many sketches.

In 1499, French soldiers used the clay horse as a target for archery practice!

The Last Supper

In 1495, Leonardo began to paint a **mural** called *The Last Supper*. It became one of Leonardo's most famous paintings.

The Last Supper covers one wall of the dining hall in a **monastery** called Santa Maria delle Grazie in Milan.

A Sea of Ideas

In 1499, Leonardo moved again – this time to Venice. The rulers of Venice had heard how clever Leonardo was and wanted him to help them defend their city from its enemies. Leonardo had many ideas for ways to improve the city's defenses, such as dams which could be used to drown invading armies! He also invented many other things, such as diving suits and flying machines.

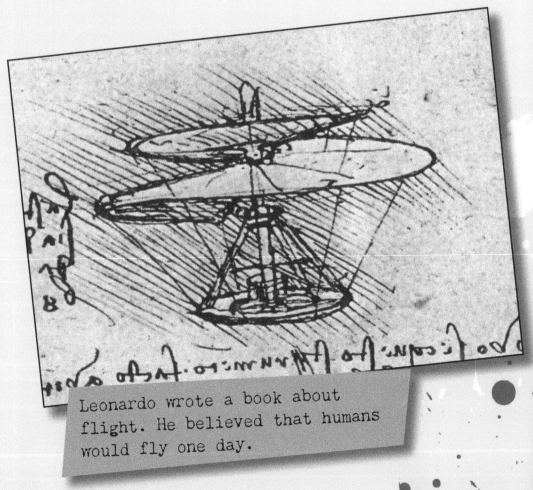

Leonardo wrote a book about flight. He believed that humans would fly one day.

Artistic Rivals

In 1503, Leonardo returned to live in Florence. Another famous artist called Michelangelo also lived in Florence at that time. They were both hired to paint a battle picture in the same room. Michelangelo had to paint a big mural on one wall and Leonardo had to paint another on the wall facing it. However, due to wet weather and other problems, the competition was never finished. Instead, Leonardo started on what was going to become the most famous painting in the world: the *Mona Lisa*.

This painting has fascinated people for centuries because of *Mona Lisa's* mysterious half-smile.

Leonardo liked to sketch parts of the human body and make notes about them. He developed the drawing technique known as the "cross section", which trainee doctors still use today.

A Man of Many Talents

In 1517, Leonardo moved to France where the King gave him a luxury house and paid him lots of money to share his ideas about science, art, architecture, **engineering** and the meaning of life. Leonardo also amused the King and his friends by building a life-sized mechanical lion. It would walk up to people and a bunch of lilies would fall out of its stomach!

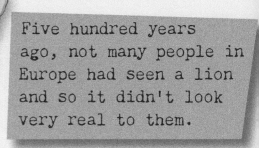

Five hundred years ago, not many people in Europe had seen a lion and so it didn't look very real to them.

stomach opens to reveal lilies

Leonardo died in 1519, aged 67. At first he was remembered only for his paintings. Then, 300 years later, people began studying his wonderful notebooks. They showed that Leonardo was not only a great artist, but also a brilliant mathematician, scientist, engineer, architect, map-maker, town planner, musician and **philosopher!**

10

Katsushika Hokusai

FACT FILE

- **Name:** Katsushika Hokusai – but he used over 30 other names during his lifetime!
- **Date of birth:** around 23rd November 1760
- **Nationality:** Japanese
- **Died:** 10th May 1849
- **Famous for:** painting and printmaking
- **Most famous works of art:** *Thirty-six Views of Mount Fuji*, especially *The Great Wave*
- **Strange but true:** Hokusai once changed his name to Gakyo Rojin Manji, which means 'The Old Man Mad About Art'

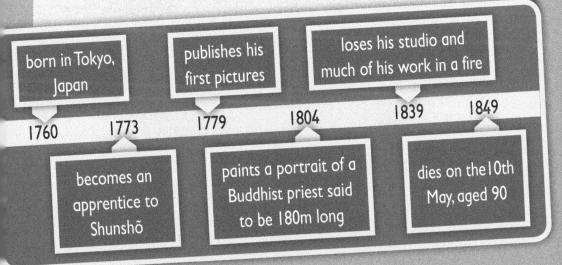

born in Tokyo, Japan

publishes his first pictures

loses his studio and much of his work in a fire

1760   1773   1779   1804   1839   1849

becomes an apprentice to Shunshō

paints a portrait of a Buddhist priest said to be 180m long

dies on the 10th May, aged 90

Making Images

Katsushika Hokusai was born in the Japanese city of Edo, which is now called Tokyo. At that time, Japan was ruled by the **shoguns.** It's thought that Katsushika's father was Nakajima Ise, who made beautiful mirrors for the shogun. Katsushika began painting when he was six years old. He may have learned to draw and paint by watching his dad paint designs on the frames of mirrors.

The shoguns ruled Japan using force, and sealed the country off from the rest of the world. Most Japanese people knew nothing about the big wide world beyond their country!

Tokugawa Yoshinobu was the last shogun of Japan.

Pictures of the Floating World

When he was 12 years old, Katsushika worked at a public library for a year. Then, in 1773, he became an apprentice woodblock cutter and **engraver**. He went on to work for Shunshō, a master of the art of ukiyo-e.

Ukiyo-e means "pictures of the floating world". The prints and paintings were meant to show beautiful moments that last for just a few minutes, hours or days. Ukiyo-e pictures were designed to make people happy.

Ukiyo-e pictures usually showed rich people or actors entertaining people.

Katsushika worked in Shunshō's studio for ten years. When Shunshō died in 1793, Katsushika began trying out other styles of art.

Wrapping Paper

When Katsushika was alive, it was common for Dutch traders to smuggle banned goods into Japan. But Katsushika was more interested in the wrapping paper they came in. The traders often wrapped goods in copies of great works of art by Dutch artists like Rembrandt and Jacob van Ruisdael.

Katsushika was amazed and inspired by Dutch paintings, like Jacob van Ruisdael's *The Wheatfield*.

Katsushika was known for his strange behaviour. The second he finished one picture, he would throw it to the floor and begin another. His studio often became so cluttered with work that he could hardly move!

Ordinary Life

Katsushika moved away from painting rich people and actors (the usual subjects of ukiyo-e). He began painting landscapes, and ordinary people doing ordinary everyday things. He also began teaching his own students. During the next ten years, his fame spread far and wide.

Katsushika was really interested in natural settings, and the way people behaved when they were outdoors.

Katsushika drew thousands of **manga** sketches, showing landscapes, flowers and animals. The style of these drawings influenced the manga characters that we know today.

Highs and Lows

During the 1830s, Katsushika produced his most famous collection of work, *Thirty-six Views of Mount Fuji*. It was so popular with the Japanese people that he added ten more pictures.

The Great Wave Off Kanagawa, is probably the most famous picture from *Thirty-six Views of Mount Fuji*.

Chicken's Feet

Katsushika enjoyed showing off. Once, when he got the chance to paint for the shogun, he placed a piece of paper on the floor and painted it blue. Then, he dipped a chicken's feet in red paint and let the bird run across the painting! He told the shogun that the picture showed maple leaves floating down a river.

If Katsushika didn't have a brush handy, he would paint with anything, including his fingers, a bottle, an egg ... even a cucumber!

Money? Who Needs it?

Katsushika regularly paid shopkeepers' bills by handing them money without counting it. No wonder he was often broke! During the Japanese famine of 1836, he swapped paintings for food.

Disaster Strikes

In 1839, Katsushika's studio was destroyed in a fire. The fire also destroyed much of his work. But Katsushika carried on painting until he died, aged 90. Soon afterwards, Japan opened up to the rest of the world. Art dealers began **exporting** lots of Japanese prints to Europe, where a whole new set of people went crazy for Katsushika's work!

HOKUSAI
Retrospektive

26. August – 24. Oktober 2011
Martin-Gropius-Bau Berlin

Niederkirchnerstr. 7
10963 Berlin
Tel. +49(0)30 254 86-0
Mi–Mo 10 – 20 Uhr,
Dienstag geschlossen

U-Bahn Potsdamer Platz,
S-Bahn Anhalter Bahnhof /
Potsdamer Platz, Bus M29, M41
Online-Tickets:
www.gropiusbau.de

Berliner Festspiele

Katsushika's paintings are shown all over the world.

Rosa Bonheur

FACT FILE

- **Name:** Marie-Rosalie Bonheur
- **Date of birth:** 16th March 1822
- **Nationality:** French
- **Died:** May 25th 1899
- **Famous for:** animal paintings and sculpture
- **Most famous works of art:** *Ploughing in the Nivernais* and *The Horse Fair*
- **Strange but true:** Rosa had a pet sheep that lived on the balcony of her family's sixth floor flat

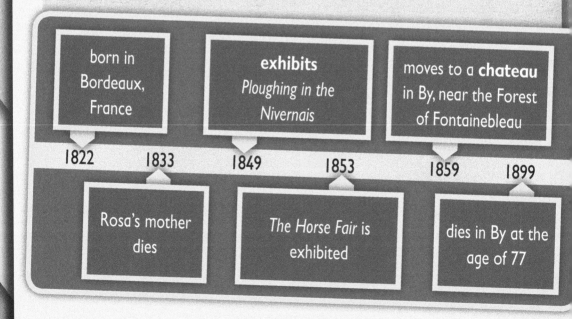

born in Bordeaux, France

exhibits *Ploughing in the Nivernais*

moves to a **chateau** in By, near the Forest of Fontainebleau

1822   1833   1849   1853   1859   1899

Rosa's mother dies

The Horse Fair is exhibited

dies in By at the age of 77

The Animal Alphabet

Rosa Bonheur was born in the French city of Bordeaux. Her dad was an artist and taught all of his children to draw and paint. Rosa loved to paint animals. When she was having problems learning to read, her mum told her to draw an animal for each letter. Rosa learned the letters in no time!

Naughty Rosa

In 1833, Rosa's mum died, leaving her dad to bring up his four children alone. He sent Rosa to boarding schools but she was always in trouble. Finally, when Rosa was 12 years old, her dad decided to teach her to become a painter.

Portrait of Rosa as a young girl by Jean-Baptiste-Camille Corot.

Rosa was expelled from one boarding school after getting her classmates to "gallop" over the head teacher's rose garden!

Learning at Home

Once she was back home again, Rosa began her training by copying other people's drawings and paintings. She visited the Louvre Museum and copied old master paintings, which she sold to help pay the family bills. She also visited nearby farms to paint and draw the animals.

Rosa would stay in the Louvre Museum from early morning until it shut. Her favourite artists to copy were Nicolas Poussin and Paul Potter.

Rosa visited **abattoirs** as well as farms to study and sketch animals in great detail.

When Rosa was 19 years old, she exhibited and sold a painting called *Rabbits Nibbling Carrots* as well as some drawings of goats and sheep. Her career as an artist had begun!

First Masterpiece

Rosa's fame soon began to spread. The French government knew she was very talented, and asked her to paint a picture of French farmers. The picture was called *Ploughing in the Nivernais*. When it was exhibited in 1849, people were amazed at how realistic the animals looked.

The French government paid Rosa to paint *Ploughing in the Nivernais*.

Doing It Her Way

Rosa lived at a time when women had few rights, and they were not able to go to art school. Rosa was determined to do things her way. She dressed like a man, cut her hair short and smoked cigars. Dressing like this meant that she could visit rough places to make sketches, such as abattoirs. She also visited horse markets to prepare for her next **masterpiece**.

Fame and Fortune

Rosa painted a huge painting called *The Horse Fair* which was exhibited in 1853. This stunning painting became the French people's favourite.

Rosa painted *The Horse Market* to prepare for painting her masterpiece, *The Horse Fair*.

By 1860, Rosa was famous in Europe and the USA. Everyone wanted to talk to her, from famous painters to royalty. American shops even sold "Rosa Bonheur" dolls, dressed in men's trousers. Rosa used her riches to buy a huge chateau and all the pets she'd ever wanted, including bulls, monkeys, an eagle and two lions, which she liked to play with!

Rosa had a pet otter, which often climbed out of its tank and snuggled down in one of the chateau's big comfy beds!

War!

In 1870, France went to war against the German state of Prussia. Rosa was ready to fight for her country and tried to get her neighbours to fight the Prussians too. She also made a plan to paint, then eat, all of her beloved animals rather than have them fall into enemy hands! However, the Prussians won and, much to her annoyance, several of their officers ended up staying in her house.

Prince Friedrich of Prussia ordered his soldiers not to damage anything in Rosa's chateau because she was so famous.

After the war, Rosa began painting wild animals such as lions, leopards and tigers. She continued to work on animal sketches and paintings for the next 40 years.

The Wild West

Rosa was always fascinated with the USA. In 1889, she painted the famous American showman Buffalo Bill Cody, when his Wild West Show was on tour in France. Her picture of Buffalo Bill sitting on his white horse became one of her most famous paintings.

Buffalo Bill's Wild West Show was action packed and included gunfights, horse racing and battles between settlers and Native Americans.

After her death in 1899, hundreds of Rosa's drawings and 892 of her paintings were sold, bringing in over two million francs, which was a huge amount of money in those days. Rosa is now remembered as the most famous woman painter of the 1800s. Her paintings hang in museums from Paris to New York.

Barbara Hepworth

FACT FILE

- **Name:** Jocelyn Barbara Hepworth
- **Date of birth:** 10th January 1903
- **Nationality:** British
- **Died:** 20th May 1975
- **Famous for:** sculpture
- **Most famous works of art:** *Single Form* and *Winged Figure*
- **Strange but true:** Barbara had such strong hands that some people believed she was born to be a sculptor

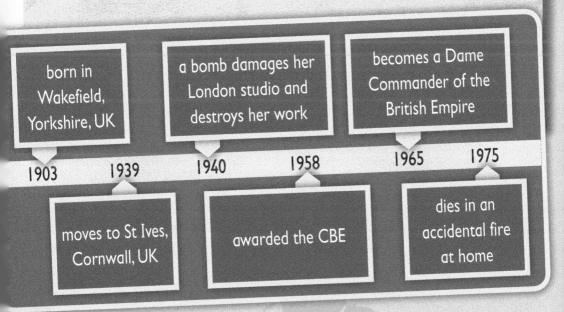

born in Wakefield, Yorkshire, UK

a bomb damages her London studio and destroys her work

becomes a Dame Commander of the British Empire

1903   1939   1940   1958   1965   1975

moves to St Ives, Cornwall, UK

awarded the CBE

dies in an accidental fire at home

Enormous sculptures

Barbara Hepworth was born in Wakefield, Yorkshire. Her dad worked for the West Riding County Council as a **surveyor** and when Barbara was little she travelled around the county with him. As her dad's car went up and down the hills, she felt like she was actually travelling over enormous sculptures!

Barbara liked the difference between the peaceful Yorkshire countryside, and the "noise, dirt and smell" of the area's "grimy" towns. It gave her ideas for creating sculptures.

No Proper Career For a "Lady"

By the age of 17, Barbara was sculpting human figures in clay and studying at the Leeds School of Art. In 1920, sculpture wasn't thought of as a suitable job for a young "lady", but she stuck at it.

At college she met Henry Moore who would also become a famous sculptor. They were really keen on "getting to grips" with their work, hacking away at great slabs of stone with chisels and mallets.

Up until the 1900s, most sculptors got other people to do much of their hard work. The sculptors made moulds of their subjects, and then paid stonemasons to do the tiring carving.

Barbara liked doing her own sculpting, seeing the stone break open to reveal beautiful shapes, colours and textures.

From Italy to St Ives

Barbara moved to London in 1921 and studied at the Royal College of Art for three years. In 1924, she went to Italy. She visited many places but mostly stayed in Florence and Rome. Italy was inspiring, and filled with art. While she was in Italy she married a sculptor called John Skeaping. They returned to England in 1926 and began to exhibit their work in various galleries. In 1929, Barbara had a son called Paul.

Abstract Art

In 1932, Barbara's marriage to John had ended and she began to live with a British painter called Ben Nicholson. They had triplets, called Simon, Rachel and Sarah. After the birth of the triplets Barbara's sculptures started to become more abstract.

Barbara with one of her abstract sculptures.

Abstract art is art that does not look like anything you can recognise. Artists make abstract art to show an idea or feeling. They are often inspired by the shapes, colours and textures around them.

Cornwall ... so Inspiring!

Barbara and Ben toured France, visiting the studios of famous artists such as Picasso. Just before the Second World War broke out, they moved from London to St Ives in Cornwall. They felt that it would be safer for their children to live there.

In 1942, the family moved to a bigger house in St Ives and Barbara was able to have a studio, where she could create new sculptures. Some of the local people thought she was strange, and that she should be cooking and cleaning instead!

Barbara was inspired by the dramatic Cornish countryside. She said that nature helped to give her new ideas, and kept her imagination alive.

The dramatic Cornish coast was an inspiration to Barbara.

Winged Figure

Barbara's hard work paid off, and businesses and organisations began to hire her to create art for them. In 1951, two of her sculptures were displayed at the Festival of Britain. Later, she was hired to make her famous *Winged Figure* sculpture for the John Lewis department store on Oxford Street, London.

Madonna and Child

In 1953, Barbara had to overcome tragedy when her son Paul was killed in an RAF plane crash. She carved the sculpture *Madonna and Child* in his memory, and it was put on display a year after his death in St Ives Church.

Barbara's sculpture *Madonna and Child*

Barbara also designed costumes and scenery for plays and operas performed on the stage in London.

Barbara in her garden at St Ives.

Death by Smoking

In 1965, Barbara, a smoker, was diagnosed with cancer of the tongue. She did not die of cancer, but her death in 1975 was caused by smoking. She was killed in an accidental fire, which started when she dropped a cigarette in bed.

In 1976, the Barbara Hepworth Museum and Sculpture Garden was opened in the house and garden where she had lived and worked. It contains a large collection of her works, which continue to inspire and impress visitors from all over the world. In May 2011, a new museum called "The Hepworth Wakefield" was opened in the city where Barbara was born.

Glossary

abattoirs places where animals are killed for food

apprentice person who learns a skill or craft from someone who is an expert in it

architecture style in which buildings are designed

bronze metal which is made from copper and tin

cast shape metal by pouring it into a mould when it is in hot, liquid form

chateau large French country house

creative use of the imagination to make something

engineering designing and building machines

engraver someone who cuts a design on to a hard surface

exhibits displays art in a gallery or museum

exporting selling goods to another country

guild group of craftsmen

manga Japanese style of cartoons

masterpiece outstanding work of art

monastery place where monks live

mural picture that has been painted on to a wall

philosopher someone who thinks about and has theories on the meaning of life

sculpture three-dimensional artwork often made from wood, stone or metal

shoguns military commanders who ruled Japan by force

surveyor person who examines, measures and values land and buildings

Index